THERE'S NO ESCAPE FROM THE LEGION
... or this book

Bill Rechin & Don Wilder

FAWCETT GOLD MEDAL • NEW YORK

Dedicated to our ladies...

Published by Fawcett Gold Medal Books, a unit of CBS Publications,
the Educational and Professional Publishing Division of CBS, Inc.

Library of Congress Catalog Card Number: 82-90884

ISBN 0-449-12461-4

Printed in the United States of America

First Fawcett Gold Medal Edition: April 1983

10 9 8 7 6 5 4 3 2 1

Bill Rechin

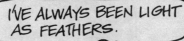

Bill Rechin

Bill Rechin

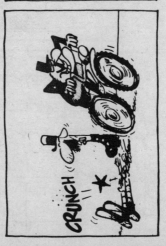

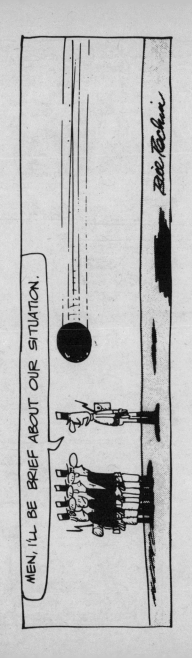

ABOUT THE AUTHORS

Artist Bill Rechin is a talented genius with a pen. His art inspires young people to say, "I could do that with a burnt match stick." In his spare time, Bill is an avid moth collector.

Writer Don Wilder is a legend in his own time. He works out of his legendary office in his legendary home in Legendville. Don says being a legend in his own time hasn't affected his life in the least.